Appoquinimink Community Library
651 North Broad Street
Middletown, DE 19709

WHAT IS ART?

Textiles

KAREN HOSACK

CHICAGO, ILLINOIS

© 2009 Raintree
a division of Pearson Inc.
Chicago, Illinois

Customer Service 888-454-2279
Visit our website at www.heinemannraintree.com

All rights reserved. No part of this publication may
be reproduced or transmitted in any form or by
any means, electronic or mechanical, including
photocopying, recording, taping, or any information
storage and retrieval system, without permission in
writing from the publisher.

Editorial: Adam Miller, Charlotte Guillain, Clare Lewis,
and Catherine Veitch
Design: Victoria Bevan and AMR Design Ltd
Illustrations: David Woodroffe
Picture Research: Mica Brancic
and Helen Reilly/Arnos Design Ltd
Production: Victoria Fitzgerald

Originated by Modern Age
Printed and bound by CTPS (China Translation and
Printing Services Ltd)

13 12 11 10 09
10 9 8 7 6 5 4 3 2 1

Library of Congress Cataloging-in-Publication Data
Hosack, Karen.
  Textiles / Karen Hosack.
    p. cm. -- (What is art?)
  Includes bibliographical references and index.
  ISBN 978-1-4109-3164-1 (hc)
  1. Textile fabrics--Juvenile literature. I. Title.
  NK8804.2.H67 2008
  677--dc22
                              2008009715

Acknowledgments
The publishers would like to thank the following for
permission to reproduce photographs:
©The Bridgeman Art Library pp. **5** (Private Collection),
6 (Musee de la Tapisserie, Bayeux, France, with
special authorisation of the City of Bayeux), **10** (Ubud
Market, Bali, 2002 (coloured ink on silk), Simon,
Hilary (Contemporary Artist)/Private Collection);
©Corbis/Sygma p. **21** (Bernard Bisson); ©David
Bygott & Jeannette Hanby p. **12**; ©Douglas Atfield
with permission from Freddie Robins p. **23**; ©Getty
Images p. **18** (AFP Photo/ Jean-Pierre Muller); ©Kaffe
Fassett p. **22**; ©Kyoto National Museum p. **20**; ©The
Metropolitan Museum of Art p. **26** (Purchase, Irene
Lewisohn Bequest, **1961** (C.**1.81.13.1**a,b); ©The
National Library of Wales p. **4** (Eirian Short); ©The
Palace Museum Bejing p. **19**; ©Courtesy and copyright
Pitt Rivers Museum, University of Oxford p. **16**; ©Polly
Hope p. **8**; ©PR ShotsPrimark p. **11**; ©Rex Features
Ltd pp. **7** (Reuters/Brian Snyder), **13** (Ray Tang), **17**;
©Sarah Jane Brown p. **24**; ©Scala Archives p. **27** (Inga
Liksaite); ©The State Hermitage Museum, Russia p. **9**;
©V&A Images pp. **14**, **15**; ©World Design Inc. p. **25**
(The Pomeroy Weavers, Kwa Zulu-Natal, South Africa).

Cover photograph of Guatemala, Chichicastenango,
Indian market, embroidered fabric reproduced with
permission of Masterfile.

Every effort has been made to contact copyright
holders of any material reproduced in this book.
Any omissions will be rectified in subsequent
printings if notice is given to the publishers.

Disclaimer
All the Internet addresses (URLs) given in this book
were valid at time of going to press. However, due
to the dynamic nature of the Internet, some addresses
may have changed, or sites may have changed or
ceased to exist since publication. While the author
and publishers regret any inconvenience this may
cause readers, no responsibility for any such changes
can be accepted by either the author or the publishers.
It is recommended that adults supervise children
on the Internet.

Contents

Any words appearing in the text in bold, **like this**,
are explained in the glossary.

What Are Textiles?

Textiles are a type of art that includes work made from materials that people weave or knit into a **fabric**. This fabric can be treated in many different ways. Some artists print onto it. Others **sculpt** the fabric or **embroider** it. This book looks at a variety of artists and **designers** who use textiles.

> The birds and landscape in this piece of textile are embroidered by hand. Every color is actually a stitch. The artist uses wool **yarns** and a needle, like a painter would use a brush and paint.

Crows by Eirian Short, 1980

William Morris

William Morris was mainly inspired by the structures of trees and plants that he saw in nature, as well as animals. His designs for textiles were used for home furnishings, such as curtains and covers. They were also used for nontextile products like wallpaper. Fashionable people at the time filled their homes with his ideas. His aim was to bring a little bit of the outside inside. Most of these items were printed by skilled **craftspeople** using carved wooden blocks. Separate patterns, called motifs, would be designed as matching repeating images, with each color being applied individually.

The Strawberry Thief by William Morris, 1883

William Morris was one of the most famous textile designers of the 19th century.

Telling a Story

This **medieval** piece of cloth tells the story of the events of the 1066 Norman invasion of England. It is a bit like a comic strip. It is not a traditional **woven tapestry**—it is actually embroidery. Like the piece on the previous page, it is created from a variety of different stitches. Some are stem stitches, which are used for the outline of the figures and the writing. Others are laid stitches, which are used for filling in the color.

Detail from the Bayeux Tapestry, c. 1082

The **yarn** used on the Bayeux Tapestry was **dyed** using vegetables, such as onion skins for the yellows.

Memory quilts

This quilt tells a story from more recent times. It was made to remember the victims and heroes of the terrorist attacks on the United States on September 11, 2001. Many people were involved in making the final quilt, as each individual section was added one by one. Some recognize the bravery of the emergency workers, while others show where the attacks took place, including the World Trade Center in New York City.

The quilt is displayed so that people can visit it and remember those who lost their lives.

Did you know?
To make a quilt, people stitch two pieces of **fabric** together with a filling in between. Many **cultures** have used this textile method to remember people and events. Can you think of any other examples?

About a family

This textile hanging shows a family with an enormous dog and three cats. It is made from various pieces of **fabric**, some patterned, some furry, and some quilted. The large parts are used as the background wall and floor. Smaller pieces of material are layered and sewn on with a method called **appliqué**.

Szekessy Family by Polly Hope, 1978

Each member of the family can be clearly recognized. Can you tell who the two parents are?

About a culture

The oldest carpet in the world was discovered in Central Asia. It is known as the Pazyryk Carpet and dates from the 5th to 4th centuries BCE. It was **woven** with great skill, which tells us that carpet-making was a respected and important trade at the time. The pictures it depicts, such as the horseman shown below, tells us how important horses were to the **culture** and day-to-day life.

Carpet (detail) by Pazyryk culture, 5th–4th centuries BCE

The ancient carpet was discovered in 1949, preserved in a layer of ice.

Ways to Decorate Fabric

A traditional way of decorating **fabric** is a method called **batik**. Hot wax is applied using a tool made from metal, to conduct heat. Skilled **craftspeople** make designs with the melted wax. When the wax is dry, the cloth is carefully put into a **dye** bath. The process of drawing with wax and dying the fabric is repeated until the whole piece is covered. The wax is removed by melting it. A cracking effect happens when dye seeps into the waxed areas.

Ubud Market, Bali, by Hilary Simon, 2002

This batik fabric was made in Indonesia.

This printed design uses two colors— purple and pink. The white of the T-shirt is used as the third color for the design. Printing is cheaper when fewer colors are used.

Using technology

A modern way to decorate fabric is to **digitally print** images and patterns. **Designers** do this by scanning a design into a computer that is linked to a special printing machine. Using this method, people can make one-of-a-kind designs or can print in bulk.

Pattern and Symbolism

Patterns in textile designs can be **symbolic** as well as just for decoration. This means that the shapes on textiles can represent things.

These African garments are known as *kangas*. They are large pieces of printed **fabric** that can be worn on the body in various ways, including on the head or as a sling for carrying a baby. The patterns can include symbols such as fruit and flowers to wish for a healthy childhood, or lions or sharks to signal danger.

KINGA NA KINGA NDIPO MOTO UWAKAPO

This *kanga* shows lamps, which are common in Africa. *Kangas* often have messages written on them. This one roughly translates as "protect the match and the fire will light."

The artist Yinka Shonibare grew up in Nigeria and Great Britain. He has taken the idea of symbolic African *kangas* and used them to create fabric sculptures. His work celebrates the fact that different **cultures** around the world have their own traditions, and asks whether some of these traditions are being lost in the modern world.

Dysfunctional Family by Yinka Shonibare, 1999

The artist who made this sculpture grew up in a mixture of cultures. Why do you think he has made these figures look like aliens?

Fashion and Pattern

Zandra Rhodes is a fashion **designer** who loves mixing lots of different patterns, colors, and **textures** together. In the 1960s she was famous for being too over-the-top. People thought that the colors and patterns she used did not go well together and felt that they could not wear her clothes. However, these days she is seen as a trendsetter and is highly respected in the world of fashion.

Coat by Zandra Rhodes, 1969

Do you think people would notice you if you wore a dress like this? How would you feel about standing out from the crowd?

New looks

In the 1960s, people began wearing clothes that were very different from what they had worn before. Today, we are used to seeing mini skirts, bikinis, and colorful printed **fabrics**, but in the 1960s these clothes were very new and daring.

It would have taken a long time to sew the beads onto this dress. They would all have been sewn individually by hand.

This 1920s dress is in two parts. Underneath, there is a plain white dress with a skirt. On top, a tunic shape decorates the outfit. The patterns on this dress have been carefully created using tiny beads. This makes the dress quite heavy. In the 1920s, women would dance wearing dresses like this one. As they moved their arms and legs back and forth, the dress would flap around. That is why it is called a "flapper" dress.

Skill and Time

It often takes a lot of skill and time to make a textile. This can make the textile very special and sometimes valuable. This apron for a girl was made in Sudan, in Africa, by a **tribe** called Dinka Tuich. It is made of two pieces of goat's skin. One is worn on the front, and the other on the back. The thin thread that holds the sides together is also made from animal skin. The apron is decorated with tiny, handmade, colored glass beads that are put in **symmetric** patterns around the edges.

Apron by Dinka Tuich tribe, 1979

Girls would wear aprons like this to perform a special dance.

Sculpting fabric
You could try changing the shape
of a piece of fabric yourself, using
a simple cloth square and a potato.
Potatoes contain starch, which will
help to keep the cloth stiff when dry.
Rub the cloth with the cut potato.
Fold the fabric into interesting
shapes and then leave it to dry
or carefully iron it flat.

The metallic silver
color of this dress is
very striking, as it
catches the bright
lights. This gives
the dress a very
modern look.

Dress by Yohji Yamamoto, 2007

Technology and geometric shapes

The Japanese fashion **designer** Yohji Yamamoto is famous for
using **fabrics** that have gone through complicated preparation.
This includes **pleating**, embroidery, and other processes that
use technology to press and stretch the material. The shapes of
his clothes are very simple, so the main focus is on the fabric
rather than other details. Because it takes so long to make
one of his garments, they are very expensive.

Clothes for Special Occasions

Everybody likes to dress up for a special occasion. Some people are able to buy special clothes from a **designer's** collection. Each spring and fall, designers from across the world show their latest clothing on **catwalks** in New York, London, Paris, Milan, and Tokyo. These clothes are usually only for individual people to order in their size. Most designers also make an "off-the-rack" line of clothes that is not as expensive.

This dress will quickly be copied by others and sold for less money in shopping malls days after being shown on the catwalk.

Dress by Tom Ford, 2000

On special occasions people sometimes like to wear costumes. Can you think of any costumes people put on for special events today? This picture shows a costume worn 200 years ago during the time of the Qing dynasty in China. Emperors at the time had the most talented artists working for them, making these beautiful costumes from the best materials available, such as gold thread, silk, and ivory. The skirt is decorated with hundreds of handmade beads and has a pattern of crashing waves along its hem.

On special occasions people like to wear clothes that fit the celebration.

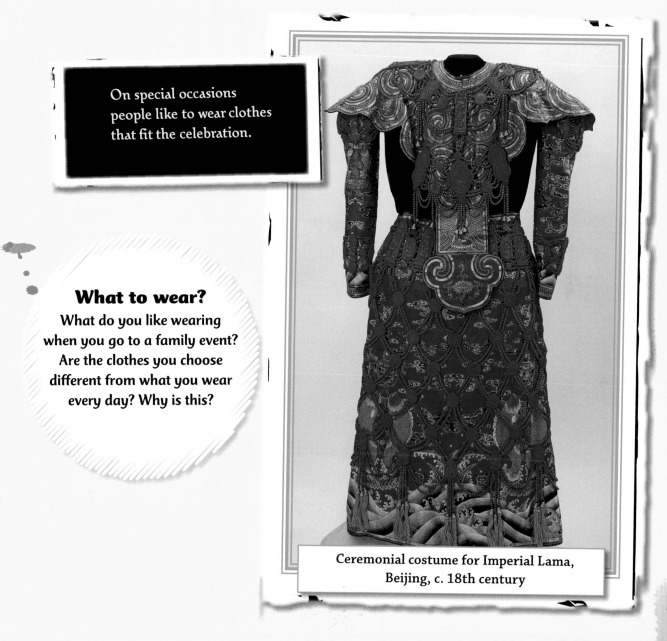

What to wear?
What do you like wearing when you go to a family event? Are the clothes you choose different from what you wear every day? Why is this?

Ceremonial costume for Imperial Lama, Beijing, c. 18th century

Identity

Can what people wear tell us about who they are? In Japan in the Edo period (1603 to 1868), everyone knew that a woman who wore the dress below was extremely wealthy and important. Each of the items that make up this 12-layered costume has evolved in design over many centuries and can be individually named. The whole dress is made from the finest silk, with hand-painted designs on the back and "kake-obi," which is worn across the shoulders.

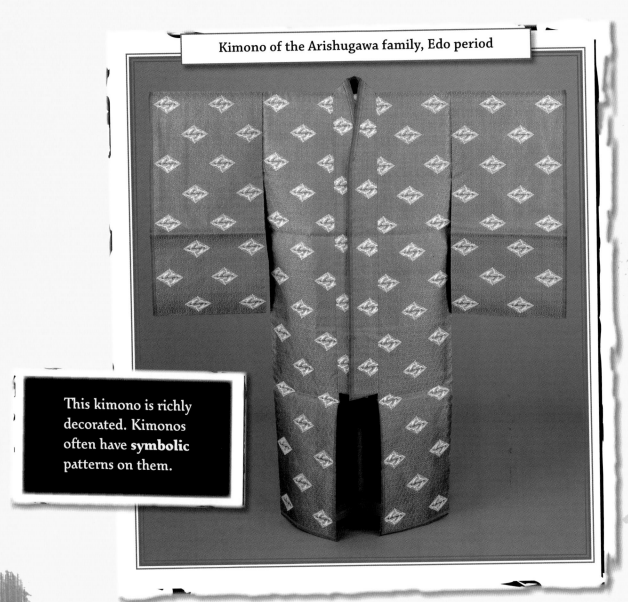

Kimono of the Arishugawa family, Edo period

This kimono is richly decorated. Kimonos often have **symbolic** patterns on them.

Think about it!
Do you have any clothes you wear to show your personality? What do those clothes say about you?

Do people who wear these T-shirts want to be different, or do they want to fit in with a group?

Today, people can show their **identity** through their everyday clothes. They might do this by wearing a T-shirt with the name of a band on it, or perhaps a political or environmental **slogan**. Some people try to show their personality by dressing like people they admire. Other people like to dress in a way that makes them stand out from the crowd, making them seem like people with their own personal style.

Knitting

The U.S. **designer** Kaffe Fassett visited Scotland and was inspired by the different colored wool **yarns** there. Afterward he decided to teach himself how to knit. The way he knits and the beautiful rich patterns and **textures** in his designs have made many people want to learn to knit, especially young people. He is most famous for his hand-knitted **commissions**, but he also designs patterns for machine knits and weavings.

China Clouds by Kaffe Fassett, 1985

This patterned cardigan is both very striking and very comfortable and warm.

Needles or machine

People can knit by hand, using a pair of knitting needles, or use a machine. A machine is much faster, but knitting by hand can get more individual results.

The small details on these houses, such as the window frames, have been sewn on top of the knitting.

Knitted Homes of Crime by Freddie Robins, 2003

Knitting can be used to create sculptures, too. These houses are knitted in wool. Each house is different. Some are country cottages, others are townhouses. The artist selected all these houses for a specific reason that adds a message to her work. She researched the types of houses that women murderers had lived in. How does knowing this make these cozy homes seem to you now?

Unusual Materials

People do not always have to knit with wool. Knitting can also be done with lots of different materials, including wire. The artist who makes these knitted wire animals uses a knitting machine. She threads the machine up in the same way as someone would when making a sweater or wool hat. It is a bit more like making a wire fence. Once the artist has knitted a piece of wire, she removes it from the machine and **molds** it into the correct shape.

This artist has made knitted sculptures of many different animals. When they are finished they can still be moved into different shapes and positions.

Scottie Dog by Sarah Jane Brown, 2006

These baskets are made from **recycled** telephone wire. The wire has been **woven** together.

Gone!
Nobody can make these wire baskets anymore. New technology means that the type of wire the men used is no longer available.

Basket by the Pomeroy Weavers, c. 1990s

Wire baskets

These baskets were made in South Africa by men who were nighttime security guards in the 1990s. The men had time on their hands and knew how to make baskets. They used the waste telephone wire they found around the buildings they were guarding. Telephone wire is very flexible, so the men developed a way of making the wire into spirals. This made it easier to work with.

Different Textiles

Throughout this book we have looked at how different artists and **designers** from different **cultures** have used textiles in their work. We have seen how various ways of decorating and changing cloth and **yarns** can have unusual effects, and how it is possible to use a range of materials to create textile pieces.

Robe à la française, 1740

This 18th-century dress would have been made by hand for a wealthy, fashionable woman. The unusual shape is achieved by wearing a tight corset and undergarments that make the skirt stick out.

Over the years, technology has changed the way that artists and designers make textiles. Artists have gone from using simple animal skins and **dyeing** processes to more complex methods like **digital printing**. It is now possible to mix and match textile designs around the needs and interests of the person who is producing the work.

This digital image has been printed onto **fabric**. It could be made into a garment, hung on a wall as a work of art, or used to make soft furnishings such as cushions.

These two examples show clearly that beautiful pieces can be created in textiles, whether the artist is using modern or more traditional methods.

Timeline

Where to See Textiles

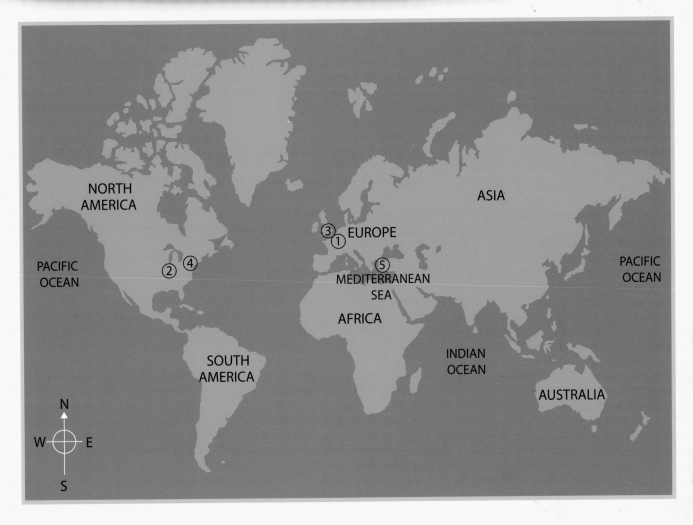

This map shows where some of the textiles in this book can be seen.

① Bayeaux, Normandy, France
   The Bayeaux Tapestry

② Kent State University Museum, Kent, Ohio
   Robe à la française

③ London, England
   See the William Morris Gallery for many examples of his work.

Visit the Victoria and Albert Museum to see costumes and fashion through the ages.

④ Metropolitan Museum of Art: The museum's Costume Institute has an extensive collection of fashion through the ages, including Tom Ford's work

⑤ Turkey is home to many beautiful textiles and carpets.

Glossary

appliqué sewing cut-out fabric onto other fabric

batik traditional way of decorating fabric using hot wax

catwalk platform at fashion shows where models walk and show clothes

commission when artists are asked to produce work for money

craftsperson skilled person who makes things

culture customs of a particular time and group of people

designer person who makes the plans for things that are made

digitally print way of printing using computer software

dye change the color of a material

embroider decorate cloth with needlework

fabric woven, knitted, or felted material

identity being an individual person

medieval from the time of the Middle Ages

mold move into shape

pleating folded and flattened fabric

recycle convert waste into something that can be used again

sculpt make a piece of art from a solid material

slogan phrase that is easy to remember and repeat

symbolic something that represents something else

symmetric being the same on both sides

tapestry material with a woven and sometimes also embroidered design, usually hung on a wall

texture way a material feels

tribe special group or family

woven fabric made by passing threads over and under each other

yarn thread used for weaving or knitting

Learn More

Books to read

King, Hazel. *Dyes and Decoration (Trends in Textile Technology)*. Chicago: Heinemann Library, 2008.

King, Hazel. *Fashion (Trends in Textile Technology)*. Chicago: Heinemann Library, 2008.

Spilsbury, Richard. *Tapestries and Textiles (Stories in Art)*. New York: PowerKids, 2008.

Thomson, Ruth. *What Are Textiles? (Art's Alive)*. Mankato, Minn.: Sea to Sea, 2006.

Websites to visit

Explore the textile collection of New York City's Metropolitan Museum of Art

www.metmuseum.org/Works_of_Art/antonio_ratti_textile_center

The Metropolitan Museum of Art's Costume Institute has a large collection of fashion and costumes through the ages

www.metmuseum.org/Works_of_Art/the_costume_institute

Find out about the history of fashion

www.designerhistory.com

Index

Appoquinimink Community Library
651 North Broad Street
Middletown, DE 19709

J
746
H

BC#33910043434589 $19.25

Hosack, Karen
Textiles

app
06/02/10